LETTERS

JONBEYOND

To order additional copies of this book, contact:
Xlibris
844-714-8691
www.Xlibris.com
Orders@Xlibris.com

ISBN: Softcover   978-1-6641-2776-0
        Hardcover   978-1-6641-2777-7
        EBook   978-1-6641-2775-3

Library of Congress Control Number: 2020916277

Print information available on the last page

Rev. date: 09/08/2022

Letters to the Self

A time to write

Chapter: 1

From whence it comes

by <u>Jonbeyond</u>

Night is the dawn of the ether worlds day
Where visions appear from the inward way
Now what I hear and what I see:
Cometh forth from what dreams in me

Sincerely,
I am another world

Chapter: 2

Depressed

by <u>Jonbeyond</u>

Can't get these thoughts out of my head
My mind has abandoned my body to bed
What day it is matters not to me
Lost in my mind wandering aimlessly

I can't get THEM to leave me alone!

Hurricane emotions have crashed me into the inner zone
I seem to have awakened in the midst of emotional debris
Dream walking in some....past....present....illusional....fantasy

Why is tomorrow always yesterday?

I have the look of one that sees within
Conscious not of now but then
Pondering questions in my mind
Seeking answers of a desired kind

Facing judgements of self persecution
Locked away in my cell of isolation
Doing time of undetermined duration

Outside my cell are partial faces
Vague are the sounds that seem like voices
Hard to hear
Dim to see
Please go away
Just leave me be

SANCTUARY this CELL has become
Safety now from everyone
Save the one who HAUNTS my mind
Who knows not day or time

I VOICE my THOUGHTS for HIM to HEAR
maybe he KNOWS the WAY out of HERE

Those WITHOUT, REGARD me STRANGE
It has been this way, SINCE my CHANGE

I THINK more NOW than EVER before

Because of THIS

The PAST has BECOME an OPEN door
For me to PEER in time and time again
To GLEAN the TRUTH of what was THEN

Now I know what
I SEE
Means for others to say.... The closed eye opens the mind
To see thru the night into the day

Though I KNOW that I will NEVER be the SAME
I will RAISE this FLESH and LIVE AGAIN

I now SPEAK from ANOTHER MIND
CONJURED up from EXPERIENCE and TIME

What was HURT has GONE away
Now that the NIGHT has become the DAY
The CURE was only for ME to SEE
The WAY of LIFE is MYSTERY

To LIVE and LEARN is the WAY
To KNOW what TRUTH has to SAY

Those who FALL in IT

Will be RAISED AGAIN

Sincerely,
My HEAD is HIGH AGAIN

A softening of the heart

Chapter: 3

Forgiveness

by <u>Jonbeyond</u>

HOW can I ever FORGET?
My LIFE was forever CHANGED
I came to KNOW great SUFFERING
My TOMORROWS are always YESTERDAY

And it is.... ALL.... because of ....YOU!

How DIRE to be HELD in the GRASP of the INESCAPABLE

What's the DIFFERENCE between a FOOL and a SAINT?:

They both BELIEVE to their own HURT

Those who DIE in TRUTH are RAISED AGAIN

I SEE with EYES from YESTERDAY
Something from the PAST, turns the EYES to look WITHIN
To look upon the ONCE WAS, time and time AGAIN

THAT which I was FORCED to RECKON with
Has left ME forever CHANGED
What I ONCE was
I can NEVER be again

The WALKING DEAD is my FATE

Who but an ENEMY would do this to ME?

A DAY of MISERY is soon FORGOTTEN
At the END of its DAY
But when it LASTS LONGER than a DAY it becomes....SUFFERING
YEARS make what is called... LONG SUFFERING
When....NO.... NUMBER.... is given to its.... END

Is HELL the GATEWAY to HEAVEN?

MUST the TRUTH always be SUFFERED for?

I can't LIVE until I have DIED?

How can LIFE come from DEATH?

This DEATH can't be the DEATH of the FLESH
Or I would BE no more

Does my SPIRIT have this POWER
To DIE and to be RAISED AGAIN?

Could this LONG SUFFERING be the state of the WALKING DEAD?:

The SPIRIT lost to TODAY, trapped in the PAST
HELD in BONDAGE by WHAT was THEN:

To LIVE the PAST is to WALK the DEAD

WHEN the SPIRIT LEAVES something it is said to be DEAD
So too....WHEN it ENTERS INTO something it is said to LIVE

HOW can the TROUBLED SPIRIT come to KNOW REST?

WHEN does a MEMORY ....HURT....NO MORE?

WHAT....MAKES.... me FEEL the WAY I do?

Is it these THOUGHTS that I REHEARSE over and over IN my MIND?

If THEY were NO MORE....
Would I BE.... ANOTHER ME?

I choose DEATH to these THOUGHTS

I give THEM up

I FORGIVE

For the SAKE of LIFE

Sincerely,
I CAN LOVE AGAIN...

Chapter: 4

Tears

by <u>Jonbeyond</u>

We are the herald of joy and despair
We are the rain from the broken hearted
We are the mist of fond memories
We are the downpour of pain

The dark clouds of emotions, summon us
The reddened eyes set us free

We are the monsoon of the emotional season

Why is the first sign of life the newborn's cry?

The Lord replenishes the earth with the rains from heaven
Does that mean that He cries for the welfare of the planet?

The oceans attest to the depth of His love

No life can survive without His tears
He cries for us all far and near
The mothers milk for the suckling child
The life's blood for all that is wild

Something as simple as what is wet
Can get to places where nothing else can get
Amazing also is it to understand
That before the force of them ... nothing can withstand

No shape can escape their imitation
It seems that tears are good for all situations
Remember your first great accomplishment
Then there was the pain of great disappointment
What about the time of great surprise
That made them flow from your eyes?

They seem to go hand and hand with what we call love
Coming when needed from our God above
So much is His love for me
That His tears make up my majority
Truly they are the life of me
Behold liquid immortality

They make up what is called trinity:
The wet
The frozen hard
A mist of floating mystery

I now know what is really strong:

The soft and yielding that never break
And can assume any shape

Amazing these things called tears
They have been around for countless years
They help the hurt to see another day
They even wash the pain away

It doesn't hurt to say again
That tears can also be your friend
They were first you knew as the newborn who cries
And the last for those that lived and died

Sincerely,
Jesus wept

Chapter: 5

You Tell Me

by <u>Jonbeyond</u>

I would like to pose challenge to you...
The way it works is that I give you clues...
From truthful self confessions of myself...
I want you to tell me who I am...

Medium defines me
The power of conjuration
Spiritual ether
Gateway to when's and where's
How to's

Submit yourself to me

I exist but to serve
Thru the willful submission of you:
Does the purpose of my being become manifest

I am what I am
I am the slave that serves his master
In any way that he conceives to use me
I can be sent on any mission
That my master has knowledge of
I serve my masters truth in how it is expressed
I am the slave that can be served to one's own benefit
If I have been conceived to serve as such

His will is my will

I speak with no voice
I am perceived by sight
Comprehended by sound
Sensed by touch

Thru your submission:
You can become one with long dead masters
Whom I did serve

I am the immortal slave
Whose will it is:
To serve the will of the master who willed me

Be warned:

To look upon the willed one
Is to be subject to the will of the one who willed him

Though I am neither good or evil
By any will of my own:
I serve without prejudice

I am the Jinn of imagination
Your will is my command
Any place
Anything
Anytime
What ever you think of ...
I will be that for you

From earliest time:
I have been crafted by the hand
Guided by the mind

Those who submit their self to me:
Receive all that I am

I have the power thru servitude:
To transport...enlighten...direct...amuse
Whatever is my master's will

By this time, you must know who I am
Ever hear the expression:
Can't see the forest for the trees
How true that can be in this situation

Sincerely,
The obediant servant

Chapter: 6

Self Esteem

by <u>Jonbeyond</u>

Why was I born this way?
Would it have been better
If I had not known a day?
Will it always be worse
and never better?

Seems like I am on punishment
All the things I want seem to be absent
Hard to hold my head up high
Of all I have...none is pride

I am the dust of the earth

Not like others is this self called me
What they have, I see not in me
In some former life, did I commit some great sin?
That made me into this alien

Why do mirrors keep telling me
That they look better than what I see?

Why are these thoughts in my mind?
That tell me that I am not their kind

Weak is the voice I use to speak
The weight of doubt makes me feel so weak
My head is bowed and rare to rise
Avoiding the glare of glaring eyes

My thoughts say they think small of me
I find it hard to disagree
I wish I could forget my sins against myself
that make me feel less than everyone else
It's bad enough what they do
Why would I do it too?

How many times have I called myself names?
The very ones that they said the same
That seems to be proof to me
That I am as bad as I think myself to be

What is it that I just said?
Something about thoughts in my head

AMAZING!

Something has just dawned on me
Would I feel better if I thought better of me?
Am I really so different from everyone else?
They like I search for self

The conflict was always inside of me
Searching for what I could agree

Hope is not lost when there is at least one friend
Make sure for yourself that it is the one within

A friend is one who shares of himself
In all the world there is no greater wealth
Truly rich is the one
When conflict in the self is finally done

Behold the glow that radiates from within
When one has secured the internal friend
With the light of my own thoughts to light my way
What my brother has leads me not astray
With wealth of my own
what is there to bemoan?

You are you and I am me...
What is there left to envy?
I thank the Lord for what is given
With peace inside, one has a life worth living

Each day is new and full of treat
When one knows that for true love...
One does not have to compete

Sincerely,
I love me some me

Writing Prompt
Write a poem about a flaw that you see in yourself.

A father sees himself through his child

Chapter: 7

I Love You

by <u>Jonbeyond</u>

The way we know that this life is real
Is by the fact that we can feel
There is a truth that I can testify
We need someone to care in order to survive

I have come to know from feeling pain
That to deeply care is much the same
But in a way that leaves one high
Because of how good we feel inside

It's because of you

I thank my mom for giving birth to me
And my dad who in me I see
I can't remember when I first did walk
Nor the time when I first did talk
Or the time of my first meal
Nor how it was to be held did feel
Nor the fact that you were the reason why
I smelt of oil and was clean and dry

My first smile is unknown to me
Thanks to you, it came to be

In time to come, I began to run around
Discovering a world where wonders abound
Experiencing all kinds of joys
Playing with people and toys

Then I knew what it was to be sad
When my hide was tanned for being bad
But that did not last for long
When I was kissed and hugged and schooled of right and wrong

My first day of school was one of fear
You went away and left me there
But that went away in the end
When I began to make new friends
Some were fun in talk and play
Others I wished would go away
This is life I began to see
All is not fun and full of pleasantries

Never the less life was good
When I found her in my neighborhood
She made life a greater joy
Something better than playing with boys

Then I knew what it was to lose my mind
Thinking of someone else all the time
Mom said I had the symptoms of
something that our God calls love
My dad began to laugh at me
Boy, with that girl, you ought to be

The Lord blessed us both to feel the same
We shared our time till marriage came
Then came a joy from up above
A child...the product of our love

Now all the things I could not remember
I see now thru my families youngest member
I see all myself in her
All the things that once were

No words can describe all the joy I feel
For this life that love made real

I can't help but to shed some tears
That my child might know pain and fears
But there is one thing that I am certain of...

She will always have my love

Sincerely,
Something we all need

Chapter: 8

Meekness

by <u>Jonbeyond</u>

The Good Lord is said to have come for the weak
The truth is that He came for the meek
The state of the world and all that is wrong
is the result of the deeds of the unmeek strong

May the Good Lord bless all that are meek
For He is a shepherd and they are His sheep
He guards them in both the night and the day
From all type of predator who would make them PRAY

The Lord is the strength of the meek!

What is strength when it is not tempered by the cool fire of meekness?
Is it not: ... a force of destruction ...
An abuse of love and respect ...
A selfishness that serves only one ...
A blindness that would make a lie the truth ...?

The meek strength of the Lord is like unto the ocean of the earth:
Yielding as it is: ...
It can neither be overcome or destroyed by none
Upon it all life depend ...
Yet to the greatest...and to the least ... it will bend

It asketh nothing ...
But giveth all ...
Is this not like the Lord that came for the meek?

How long has the ocean served this earth?
It has been the breast milk for all God's children from birth
The meek strength of the Lord will bend but not break
It is a false strength for those who know not to give
But only to take ...

The Lord said: "I will come again"...
Is He not like the grass of the earth?
Which sustains the wild beast
Who are our
Food
Friend and Servant

What strength is greater than this:?
A guardian that is food for all He protects
He lays down His life to save
He riseth again to lead
There is no end ... to His good deeds

It is the unmeek strong that prophesy the end of the world
The meek strong prophesy the again coming of the Lord
Which is like the new growth of spring:
There is no death ...
Only come again ...

See the difference between the unmeek strong and the strong meek

Yeah ...
The meek shall inherit the earth!
For they shall come again ...
For the way of the Lord is everlasting life:

If I die before I wake
I pray the Lord my soul to take
Because I know that if I am with Him ...
I will surely come again!

Sincerely,
The STRENGTH of meekness

Chapter: 9

Best Friend

by <u>Jonbeyond</u>

TWAS THE SUMMER OF HIGH SCHOOL'S END
THAT I FIRST ENCOUNTERED MY BEST FRIEND

IT WAS HE WHO CAME TO ME
HOW THE FRIENDSHIP CAME TO BE

LET'S RUN TOGETHER...

HE SEEMED TO KNOW THINGS THAT I DIDN'T
DOING THINGS THAT I WOULDN'T

NEVER AT A LOSS FOR WORDS
THE MORE HE TALKED THE MORE I HEARD

THEN SOMEHOW IT CAME TO BE
THAT I WOULD FOLLOW AND HE WOULD LEAD

WE WENT TO PLACES NEAR AND FAR
THANKS TO ME AND MY CAR

THERE WAS HARDLY ANY TIME
THAT HE WASN'T LEAVING SOMETHING ON MY MIND

AS A NERD, I KNEW THINGS FOR SURE
HE SAID THE STREETS HAD TAUGHT HIM MORE

THAT IS HOW IT CAME TO BE
THAT HE SAID ...THAT HE KNEW MORE...THAN ME

I HAD TO ADMIT ...THAT IT WAS TRUE
THAT PLAYING PEOPLE, I KNEW NOT TO DO

BLIND WAS I TO SEE
THAT HE WAS REALLY TEACHING ME

THERE WERE THINGS... THAT HE FOUND TO DO
I HAD TO ADMIT...THAT I LIKED THEM TOO

IT CAME TO BE...THAT WE WOULD MEET
IN GAMES AND WORDS... DID WE COMPETE

BRAGGED...HE DID...IN THE BEGIN
TILL... MY MIND... SAW HOW TO WIN

THEN HE INTRODUCED WHAT HE SAID WAS A TREAT FOR ME:
A MEANS TO TRAVEL CEREBRALLY

HE LATER CONFESSED, WHILE I FLOATED ABOVE THE TREES
THAT IT MADE IT EASIER FOR HIM TO HANDLE ME

UNKNOWN TO ME, AT THAT TIME
HE BEGAN TO BE UNKIND

I WAS VERY SLOW TO SEE
THAT WHAT MIGHT SEEM KIND... WAS MOCKERY

BLIND WAS I TO REALITY
HE WAS NOW MY ENEMY

MY GUARD WAS DOWN HE KNEW MY WAYS
HE BETRAYED ME MUCH IN COMING DAYS

LONG BEFORE, HE TOOK THE LIBERTY
TO GIVE A ...NICKNAME...TO ME

CALL ME SLOW AGAIN
HE WAS NOT MY FRIEND

OTHERS LAUGHED, I KNOW THEY DID
HE SHOWED THEM HOW I WAS LIKE HIS KID

HIS BOLDNESS CUT ME LIKE A KNIFE
WHEN I FOUND OUT HE KNEW MY WIFE

BEFORE THIS TIME HAD COME ALONG...
HE CLAIMED THERE WAS NO RIGHT OR WRONG

AT LAST... WISDOM HAD COME TO ME
WHAT HE WAS, I COULD CLEARLY SEE

THE ANGER AT FIRST, I SAW TO LET GO
MEMORIES OF US, MADE ME KNOW

FOR I THINK THAT IN HIS WAY, HE WAS MY FRIEND:
TEACHING ME OF ME IN THE END

WHAT IS A FOOL?...BUT HE WHO SEES NOT HIMSELF
BITTER MEDICINE...BRINGS ALSO BETTER HEALTH

SINCERELY,
THE LORD WORKS IN MYSTERIOUS WAYS

Chapter: 10

Abandoned Child

by <u>Jonbeyond</u>

Within us all there is a need
for the love that God decrees

What is a life that lives without?

Compassion dared to talk to me
to what end I could not see
from where I come there's no such thing
a world...that place of no caring

No one but me

Without a choice was life for me
mom and dad abandoned me
to find my way with no care
among strangers here and there

Someway somehow I managed to survive
among the truth and the lies
now no one but me I trust
I dare to do what I must

What I want is my way
I make the truth to gain my say
I don't care what they think!
life's an ocean...you swim or sink

The flames of anger keep me warm
I'll get them back!...keeps me from harm
weakness is this thing called care
the law of mine says do not share

Now here you come with your love
something that I know not of
forgive me for the things I do
I love not me...how could I you?

Within this self I feel a need
but what it is I cannot see
I knew it once long ago
but to survive I let it go

Something is wrong, I've always known
more so now, since I've grown
hard to lie to myself
love is need for someone else
first for me is the need
then to share... will set me free

At first I fought because I feared
your love for me seemed so weird
I caused you hurt you could have left
instead you stayed and only wept
the tears you cried made see
you were only saving me

Now the child feels free to cry
freed at last...from the pain inside

Sincerely,
I LOVE YOU TOO

To be abstract

Chapter: 11

Untamed

by Jonbeyond

I closed my eyes and saw infinity
The eye of the mind sees what is perceived
A mental world formed by what is believed
Inhabited by what is done habitually

I thought I was done having these thoughts
Good sense told me what I should keep and what I should not
It seems as if these thoughts have a mind of their own
Why can't I get them to leave me alone?

It seems that I have a habit

How can one escape from himself?
Does that mean to become someone else?
Or just some different way you would like to be?
Maybe a change of reality?

The only thing I can think of
Is the things we do think of

Can it be said that we are what we think?
That being so....
can we think not to think?

Now take a moment to ponder what was said

How can I not know what is in my head?

Can thought have the power of no thought?

If I turn myself off
Who will turn me back on?

Maybe it's all about looking at nothing

With nothing to see

Is there anything to think?

Now we need to know where thoughts come from
It appears they come without asking anyone

It's been my experience

Whether asleep or awake
They come and go for their own sake

Sounds like the nature of something wild
Something to be tamed and taught like a child

To control a wild horse, one must hold by the reigns
Hold on for dear life until control is gained

The wild now ordered by the rider called habitually
Behold an ordered mentality

One must be prepared to take the wild ride
If one is to achieve order inside

See how the lord works in mysterious ways
He has given you something
That if not tamed....will run away

At the same time it's your transportation to anywhere
If order is gained through habitual care

look for green pastures for your trusted steed to graze
Then will he speed you to places and leave you amazed

The more and more I believe this thing
I see that it has the coming of wings

Sincerely,
I am the calm wind

Interior Decoration

Chapter: 12

Psychosis

by <u>Jonbeyond</u>

Would you mind if I thought at you?
Seems there was much I thought I knew

That was mere illusion in my mind....

Which prompts the question....
Of what mind....am I now?

It is said, that the truth will set you free

Is this the freedom from confusion?

Or the freedom to think as you please
With respect to the present reality?

How can I know?

My primal state is all acceptance

Assimilation

Is my means of manifesting myself on the plane of my existence

Early survived experience, gives character to my being:
I am what has been done to me
And how I have reacted to it

I seek to survive by adaption
Though I speak as an individual:
I experience consciousness as a duality:

There is that which I experience from without
And that which I experience from within

There lies the dilemma

A duality that is of one accord

How can two see as one?

Who is in command?

Is there a third aspect of consciousness?
What I sense
What I remember
What I think
Not necessarily in that order

That leads to what I do

How can I not be insane?
Whatever I do speaks of he who dwells within
We reason for what I do
We look forward and behind

One is called....dreams
The other is called....memories

By these two is my future shaped
By I do what I think

Does that say I am what I think?

Coexistence demands that I show that I can relate
Else I will be regarded as strange

I must acknowledge the prevailing consciousness

Sanity is measured by this
If I differ greatly, I might be regarded as insane

It is dangerous to question the prevailing consciousness:
Men have been put to death for this
Better to blend in than to stand out

Sanctuary is the MATRIX

Thinkers are lonely people
Traveling to wherever one's thoughts might lead

When is the mind bound or free?

To be as others....or a strange enigma?
Which offers the greater comfort?

One must be brave to think alone

Either a genius....or insane

And not worry about what others think

Better to be misunderstood
Than to misunderstand

One can save himself by truth within

If strong enough:

One can save the world

Sincerely,
Why do I think these things?

Chapter: 13

Grown Old

by <u>Jonbeyond</u>

Over a space of time, a story unfolds
A series of events, that marks my growing old
On occasions, I look back in my mind
Tracing my steps as I traveled thru time

O my God, look what time has done to me
No more a child but one of the elderly
I can recall distant memories, when I was young and tender
But two minutes ago, where I put something, I can't remember

The Lord in His wisdom, made it this way:

As a child I knew not the concept of time
But it was thru the duration of this, that I developed my mind
Things that happened, unremembered by me
Shaped the actor in life, I would come to be

Experiences thereafter, added to as well as took away
From the mind that grew and searched for it's way
School was everywhere and everything

To forever learn is the way of true living
Change is the ever flowing stream that carries us on without cessation:
Till we arrive at our final transformation

Behold wisdom, which is the saving development of mind:
For those who do not secure it, are lost and blind

Chance and circumstance are sudden storms that overtake us as we sail:

Some wash us ashore on islands much like paradise

Some maroon us to places we despise

This is life for those who live it
Forever changing by the minute

The body we live in has it's story to tell:
Governed by a mind, that makes life heaven or hell

Chance and circumstance lay hand on it as well:

A perishable vessel, indeed the body is
From infancy onwards, it faces the perils that confront all that live

Then comes the final chapter to this story that is told
All that live, whether...good...bad...wise or ignorant...grow old

Some minds are bright, even at this time
Others are dim and worn out by chance and circumstance and time

But one thing in our minds, we should hold to be true:
The Lord patiently, waits on you

Sincerely,
My time has come

Three aspects of consciousness

Chapter: 14

Triad

by <u>Jonbeyond</u>

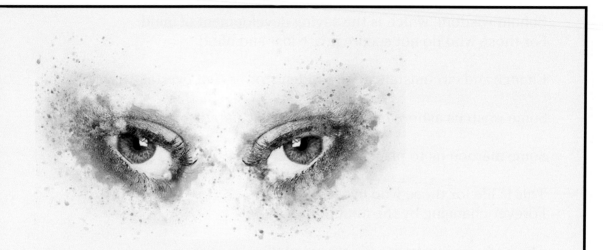

IF the floating armless busts of the three maidens,
appeared on a Tarot card... it would read like this:
the three busts represent the three emotional states of the female mind:
the three busts float, evenly spaced, from left to right:

the one on the left, with the right breast exposed,
represents the logical mind driven by emotion
the one on the right, with the left breast exposed,
represents emotion driven by logic
the one in the center, with no breast exposed,
represents the undriven, free floating self, who goes with flow

IF you picked this card...your past, present and possible,
emotional, future are represented:

you were at one time controlled by sex

now you look for the best way to have it

your best future lies in what happens naturally

Sincerely,
I found the one

Chapter: 15

Forgetfulness

by <u>Jonbeyond</u>

I seem to have forgotten what I was about to do ...
If I just give it some time ... maybe I will ... remember ...

I remember so clearly ... way back then ...
But a mere moment ago ... has just eluded me ...

I am so full of thought: ...

It seems that life is really a dream
How can you go to sleep ... when you never woke up?
Seems like we are all walking in our sleep ... lost in our dream ...
haven't you noticed? ... you're always thinking ...
about one thing or another

Interrupted only by the needs of the other ...

You started to do something then drifted into a thought
Carried to another place ... stargated to some then you knew
Now...where was I before? ... was I paying so little attention?

I could have sworn... I knew ... I have to remember past where I am ...

To get to where I was before ...
A dream within a dream ... I hope I don't get lost ...

Okay now ... where was I? ...
seems there was something I was about to do ...
Yeah ... it had something to do with ... damn! ...
another gate ... now where am I?
This is something that can wait ... I am wasting time ...
it shouldn't take me this long

The harder I think ... the harder it is to ...

This happened to me before ... okay ... where is here? ... give it a minute ...
You know how you are ... believe that, ... now ... I ... see ...
I have to watch my drift ... there must be some way I can avoid getting lost

Maybe if I made it a rule ... to finish what I start ... one dream at a time ...

The dream of my other should be my first priority ...
Where it is ... I should be ...

I like you have a responsibility: ... to mind my own reality ...

Sincerely,
Where is now? ...

Chapter: 16

The Gun

by <u>Jonbeyond</u>

He took ME from my MOTHER EARTH
The heat of FIRE, gave ME NEW BIRTH
I have BECOME something NEW
An AWFUL TOOL for MAN to USE

I CHALLENGE SKILL in USING ME
MAN prides HIMSELF in ACCURACY

HE TAUGHT ME what it IS to KILL
Even HIS CHILDREN.... THINK it a THRILL

The VOICE of DEATH

From the DAYS before MAN'S BIRTH
I LAY at PEACE in MOTHER EARTH
Without the NEED for eyes to SEE
All that WAS.... WAS also ME

Then HE that WALKED upon HER FACE
TORE ME LOOSE from HER EMBRACE
Then with FIRE, did HE SEGREGATE
BEHOLD me NOW the METAL STATE
From the WHICH, HARD THINGS are MADE
Now BEHOLD the METAL AGE

Always MAN is PRONE to WAR
That is what HE will USE ME for

In HIS MIND, did HE CONCEIVE
That HE would give a VOICE to ME
With HIS HANDS made HE a WEAPON
With a VOICE that sends GOOD MEN to HEAVEN

OTHERS whom HE SEGREGATED
POWDER and lead HE DELEGATED
She called POWDER is my BREATH
Her BREATHED FORTH brother....LEAD....causes
DEATH

When I SPEAK I also SPIT
BEHOLD the whole POINT of it

With every COMING GENERATION
I BECOME the NEW SENSATION
SHOWING better ways to KILL
MAN declares his growing SKILL

Should I take PRIDE that I AM the ONE
That MAN now calls the LETHAL GUN?
Seeing ME and then BEYOND
HIS vision percieves the ATOM BOMB

I CRY aloud in EVERY WAR
Just the thing that I am MADE for
I SCREAM DEATH from EVERY SIDE
I WHISPER it from SUICIDE

In DEEP THOUGHT within his ... MIND...
Will HE ECHO my VOICE to ... ALL ... LIVING KIND?

I SPEAK the END of BEAST for MEAT
I SHOUT in SPORT as men COMPETE
After all that is SAID
I CAUSE MORE than what is DEAD

I WONDER if possibly
I could be USED usefully?
In all the days of my EMPLOY
I know naught but to DESTROY

My only VIRTUE that I can SENSE
Is to be USED for SELF DEFENSE

Sincerely,
I want to LIVE

Chapter: 17

Which one?

by <u>Jonbeyond</u>

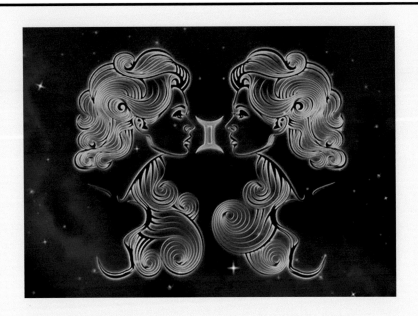

It has been said that life is a dream ...

If life is a dream ... then a dream is life ...

All you dream could be life
All your life could be a dream

    QUESTION: ...

Is it this LIFE we call a DREAM

    OR: ...

This DREAM we call LIFE?

Sincerely,
Does it really matter?

Chapter: 18

I had a dream

by <u>Jonbeyond</u>

Sleep came upon me
The mind's eye did open

I did see with sight beyond sight
As with sight that saw : forward and behind

As I saw ... so I was ... and I knew not day or time

There and where, I was :
Empowered only to behold

Sincerely,
My mind doth see

Chapter: 19

The end

by <u>Jonbeyond</u>

Word came to me that my sister was dead
I cried till my eyes were red
then my mind began to fill with thought
I thought some of what I gave her
But more of what I did not

Oh Lord why do I think this now that she's gone?
When she was alive, there was so much more we could have done

I was trying to make this rhyme, but I think talking is better

It brings tears to my eyes when I replay the memories of us
Lord knows that we were poor... but we were rich with family drama
Not having much puts you in touch with your soul ...it makes you
people first

Oh these tears are coming with every memory ...I see her at different
times of our lives...
It is pain to accept that they are only memories ...the memory of
her suffering convicts me of the crime of not doing more ...give me a

minute ... these tears are blinding me ... why do we always talk about what we should have done? ...
Im so guilty ... will I cry myself to death?

She prayed for death ... the last time I saw her, DEATH had painted her a new face

I foolishly thought that it was something that would pass away ... she had recovered before...

I saw not the truth ... HE stood in our presence ... her new face was a reflection of HIS

I wonder now, If I could have protected her if I would have stayed longer...I thought I would see her again ... there I go assuming things ...my many tears have stayed their flow for now

I feel them returning because I am remembering more of what I am guilty of ... there is so much I would change ... these tears I know now, are for me ... she is free and I have yet to go that way ... what has he in store for me?... no crime goes unpunished
may her children know that there was no greater sacrificer than your battered and tortured
mother... she left here thinking of others more than herself ... my tears are for you as well
... your tears are all you can give now ... she would have much more wanted your love

I am still trying to understand these tears ... out of the blue they keep coming ... I hope I don't have a wreck while driving ... sometimes I try to talk and I can't ... oh Lord if this is my punishment, let me cry an ocean ... but I know ... that it won't bring her back

Sincerely,
Your brother

Chapter: 20

The voice of pain

by <u>Jonbeyond</u>

I asked the Lord:

Why do we come by
The shedding of water and blood
And the feeling of pain?

I heard no answer ...
But I thought this:
There seems to be a price for everything ...

The caterpillar dies so the butterfly can live

The seed's shell casing breaks so that the plant can grow

We hail from sperm and egg

They cease to be the two ... and become the one

The soul of man has no personal voice

Until he has been stabbed in the heart of his innocence

If he survives ... a tempered soul emerges:

Pain is the first great truth

Sincerely,
The pain of truth

Does such creature exist?

Chapter: 21

The immortality issue

by <u>Jonbeyond</u>

I have not many words for this post....
It's been my experience, since becoming a new member
That you have contests where you use only a few lines
My assumption is the object is....to provoke much thought

I have a question for you that I think will do just that

An amoeba is a ONE celled ORGANISM
That PROCREATES by DIVIDING in TWO

IS one....HALF....OLDER....than the OTHER?

And if you THINK like I do, the answer is.... NO

How....OLD....would that make....ANY....AMOEBA,....that is
ALIVE TODAY?

Since posting this, I have had only two reviewers to actually address the question and attempt answer....both were right....a male and a female....HE INVISIONED the answer.... MENTALLY.... by moving the questions PARTS....but would not completely ACCEPT it....saying, there maybe MORE to it.... SHE took KNOWN KNOWLEDGE and PONDERED its LOGICAL course....SHE unlike he RESTED in HER CONCLUSION... lets PONDER this REALITY....the AMOEBA....a CREATURE whose ENVIRONMENT is WATER....THE MOST ABUNDANT RESOURCE on the PLANET....at some particular TIME goes into a STATE where HE DIVIDES into two EQUAL HALVES that are YOUNG VERSIONS of ITSELF...this is INCREDIBLE!!...he became YOUNG AGAIN!!....IMAGINE being ABLE to become a KID AGAIN and have all the KNOWLEDGE you had as an ADULT and you have been doing this FOREVER, as long as the OCEAN has been there.

Sincerely,
I WONDER

Chapter: 22

The lying TRUTH

by <u>Jonbeyond</u>

In the BEGINNING was the TRUTH and all that was
...was WHAT it was
The RESULT was PEACE and HARMONY
.... DUE to a NON-CONFLICTING unity

REALITY being TRUE or ITSELF
... a PERPETUAL RHYTHM gave LIFE to all else

TRUTH supporting TRUTHS that CAN BE
... gives BIRTH to all THINGS like YOU and ME

MAN because of his MIND
...IMPOSES a WILL of SELF-INTERESTED kind

DISCOVERING all the THINGS that he can DO
... HE seeks to IMPOSE HIS WILL on WHAT is TRUE

HISTORY records HIS RISE and FALL
... when LEADERS arise whose MINDS are SMALL

Now here WE are in the PRESENT
... The TRUTH being ASSAULTED by a LYING PRESIDENT

AIDED by modern TECHNOLOGY
... WE have ringside seats to a SUSPICIOUS REALITY

Is a LIE stronger than the TRUTH?
... In REALITY ... NO ... BECAUSE of lack of PROOF

So WHY is it taking all this TIME
... for JUSTICE to CONVICT the CRIME?

CIVILIZED MAN now CHALLENGES our PERCEPTION of REALITY
...PAINTING the PICTURE that HE wants US to SEE

HOPE is FADING for YOU and ME
...if WE turn OUR backs on SELF-HONESTY

Sincerely,
Just believe me

Chapter: 23

God of the Microverse

by <u>Jonbeyond</u>

I now bring the macroworld of the "meat sacks" to it's very knees
Bringing death and infection to all by breath and breeze

See how they wither and fade before my micro might
I wage war on them by the day and night

Their very numbers will I decimate
Until they learn how to vaccinate

On the very "meat sacks" that they are will I infect and thrive
I am amused at their efforts to destroy me so they can survive

Haven't they learned from their history's past
That the "one who becomes two" will ever last

There is one thing about the "meat sacks" I can say
There are kinsmen of mine that they hold at bay

Impressive they are with what they can create
To hold us at bay ... till alas we mutate

In the macroworld they band together to stem my onslaught
I am a multiplying horde that cannot by physical means be fought

I by "one become twoism" stand omnipresent
By this means ... I infect the entire planet

The "meat sacks" fight well against my latest romp
Save the "meat sacks" of America led by the "meat sack" called Trump

They and I share one mother by birth
Their numbers are disease to our mother earth

The reaction by Her to save Herself from their way
Appointed me antibody as I make them meat for prey

In age past I was called forth when they threatened Her breath
I wreaked havoc on their numbers and was called Black Death

Now they call me Corona as I decimate their numbers this present day
Unchecked ... my appetite for the "meat sacks" will wipe them away

They pray to their macro God to save them ... will He save them?
... maybe ... if they repent

Sincerely,
I can be slain and yet liveth

Chapter: 24

Reign on Earth

by <u>Jonbeyond</u>

On this present day
the Father of lies
presented Himself
before the Truth
and said:
I am come from
walking to and fro
on the earth and
America bids Me challenge You:
for Reign on Earth...
there is one who
has arisen
who champions my way
He is empowered
by the greedy rich and souls that are not at rest
He engorges the rich
and fans the flames of unrest...
He has become
their Truth...
the CHOSEN ONE...
He is bent
to MY WILL...
as well as

they who follow...
they cast ballots
to secure His reign...
the followers of Truth
appear weak before Him:
He uses their Loyalty to Truth and Fairness
against them

HE OPENLY SACRIFICES THEM TO HIS WILL
AND THEY LOVE HIM STILL

BETTER TO REIGN ON EARTH
THAN TO SERVE...

Sincerely,
and they said ... Make us a KING

Printed in the United States
by Baker & Taylor Publisher Services